COUNTRY GUITAR

Exclusive Distributors:
Music Sales Limited, 8/9 Frith Street, London W1V 5TZ, England.
Music Sales Pty Limited, 120 Rothschild Avenue, Rosebery, NSW 2018, Australia.

This book and all music contained therein © Copyright 1993 by Wise Publications.
Order No. AM90095
ISBN 0-7119-3166-6

Cover & cassette design by Michael Bell Design. Music arranged & recorded by Alan Warner. Music processed by Seton Music Graphics.

Music Sales' complete catalogue lists thousands of titles and is free from your local music shop, or direct from Music Sales Limited.
Please send a cheque/postal order for £1.50 for postage to: Music Sales Limited, Newmarket Road, Bury St. Edmunds, Suffolk IP33 3YB.

Your Guarantee of Quality: As publishers, we strive to produce every book to the highest commercial standards.
The music has been freshly engraved and the book has been carefully designed to minimise awkward page turns and to make playing from it a real pleasure.
Throughout, the printing and binding have been planned to ensure a sturdy, attractive publication which should give years of enjoyment.
If your copy fails to meet our high standards, please inform us and we will gladly replace it.

Printed in the United Kingdom by Caligraving Limited, Thetford, Norfolk.

WISE PUBLICATIONS
London / New York / Paris / Sydney / Copenhagen / Madrid

HAMMER-ON

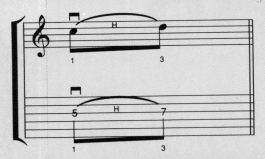

A hammer-on is where you sound a note as normal then hammer your L.H. finger down hard onto the next note.

⌒ H ⌒ means hammer-on.

PULL-OFF

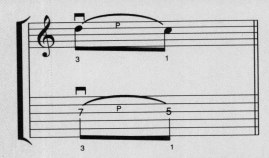

The pull-off is achieved by pulling your L.H. finger down off the string to create the next note.

⌒ P ⌒ means pull-off.

UPWARD STRING BEND

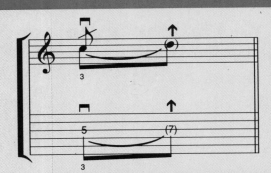

To perform an 'Upward String Bend' first strike the note, then push string up to raise its pitch. The note in brackets is the one that it will sound like. An upward string bend will normally be on the 1st, 2nd or 3rd Strings. The arrow indicates upward string bend.

DOWNWARD STRING BEND

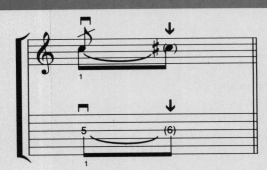

For a 'Downward String Bend', pull the string down to raise pitch. A downward string bend will normally be on the 3rd, 4th, 5th or 6th strings. The downward arrow indicates downward string bend.

SLIDE GOING UP

Strike the first note and slide up to the next.

SLIDE COMING DOWN

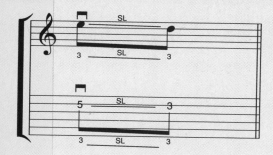

Strike the first note and slide down to the next.

TRILL

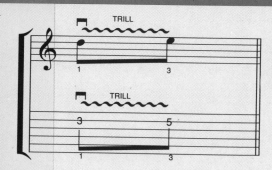

A trill effect is produced by performing hammer-ons and pull-offs in rapid succession.

RELEASE STRING BEND

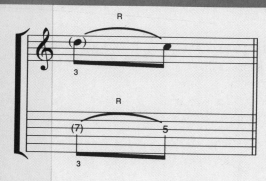

Returning bent note back to its normal position.

HOLDING THE PICK

Place your thumb over the flat part with your 1st and 2nd fingers curled underneath the pick. Hold Firmly but gently. Poise the pointed end over the strings.

Try this exercise using the pick.

= Strike down with pick

V = Strike up with pick

Try this single note melody line with the pick.

1.

*The double lines with dots tell you to repeat from the beginning.

PICK 'N' STRUM STYLE

We'll start with a couple of very basic exercises using chord shapes. The idea here is to play our original single note melody line, this time with a chord strum in between to fill out the sound. The first exercise uses the G major chord and the procedure is (1st bar):
1) Pick 6th string (single note melody line). 2) strum chord.
3) Pick 4th string (single note melody line). 4) strum chord.
Try the second bar. Keep playing these two bars over and over again for a while. Now try the next exercise using Am and Am/D chords.

PICK 'N' STRUM EXERCISES

Here are the chord shapes for the following two exercises.

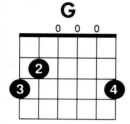
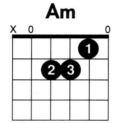
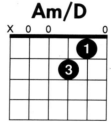

2.

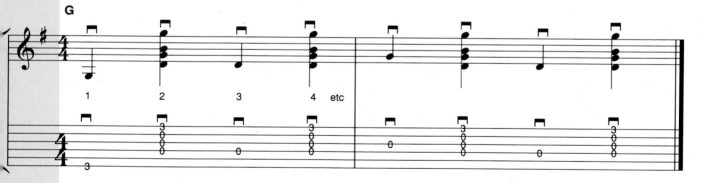

3.

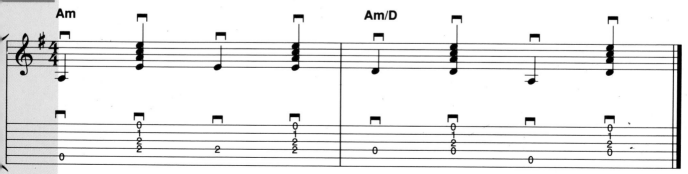

5

THE HAMMER-ON

The hammer-on technique is useful for creating a more country-type feel to the music. For this exercise first strike the open 4th string, then without striking again hammer your left hand 2nd finger down hard onto the 2nd fret of the 4th string.

4.

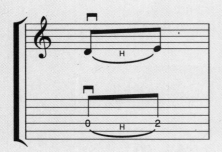

Now try the hammer-on technique in this pick and strum exercise. Hold the G chord down.
1) Pick the 6th string
2) Strum
3) Hammer-on
4) Strum
. . . and so on

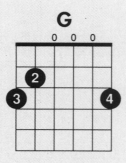

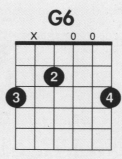

5.

These are the chord shapes for the pick 'n' strum guitar solo.

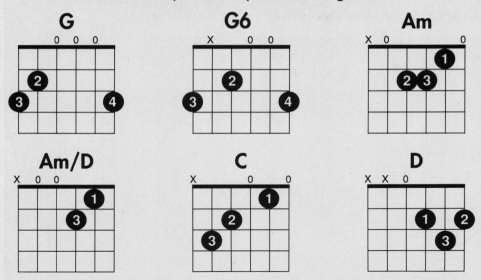

Try out the hammer-on technique in this pick 'n' strum guitar solo.
Work towards a clean sound especially on the last two bars when
changing from C to D to G. This is very much in the style of
'Tell Me Why' by Neil Young from his 'After the Goldrush' album.

6. COUNTRY PICKER

BY ALAN WARNER

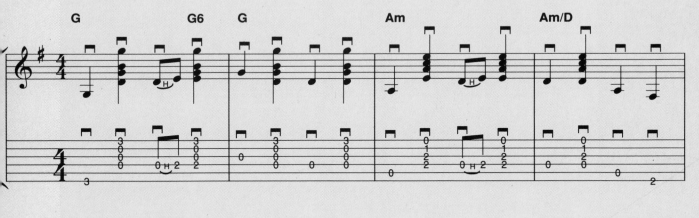

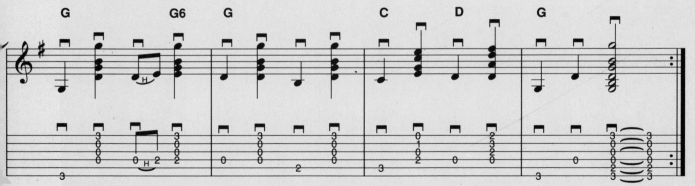

THE PULL-OFF

The pull-off is also a useful technique and like the hammer-on will help to 'countrify' your sound. This exercise shows the 2nd finger of the left hand pulling off from the 2nd fret of the 4th string onto the open 4th string. Make sure you pull downwards in a definite way to sound the second note (open 4th string).

7.

PICK 'N' STRUM EXERCISES

(USING PULL-OFFS)

These are the chord shapes for the following two exercises.

8.

9.

10. SHORT GUITAR SOLO

(USING PULL-OFFS)

BY ALAN WARNER

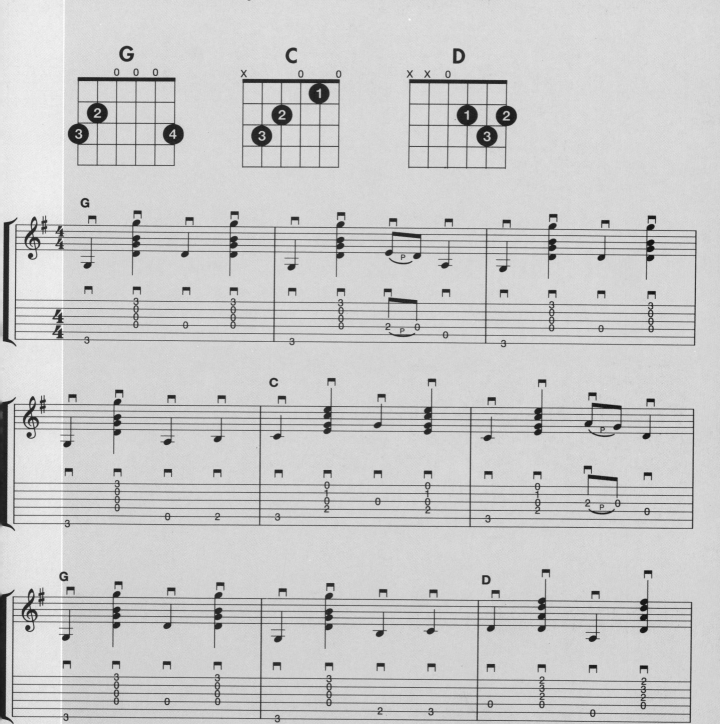

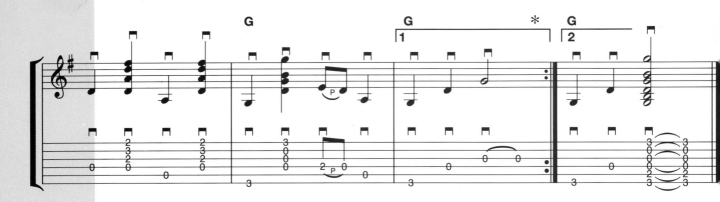

* First time around play the music in ⌐1 ⌐
When you repeat, play the music in ⌐2⌐ to finish the piece.

CHARLIE PRIDE (LEFT) AND JOHNNY CASH (PICTORIAL)

‘MISTY MOUNTAIN’

BY ALAN WARNER

The most difficult thing about this guitar solo is the F chord shape
which is used throughout, so you may need to spend some time on
this before learning the whole piece.
Also study the C (G bass) chord shape; all you do here is transfer
the C bass note (3rd fret of 5th string from the C chord) to the
G bass note (3rd fret of 6th string.)

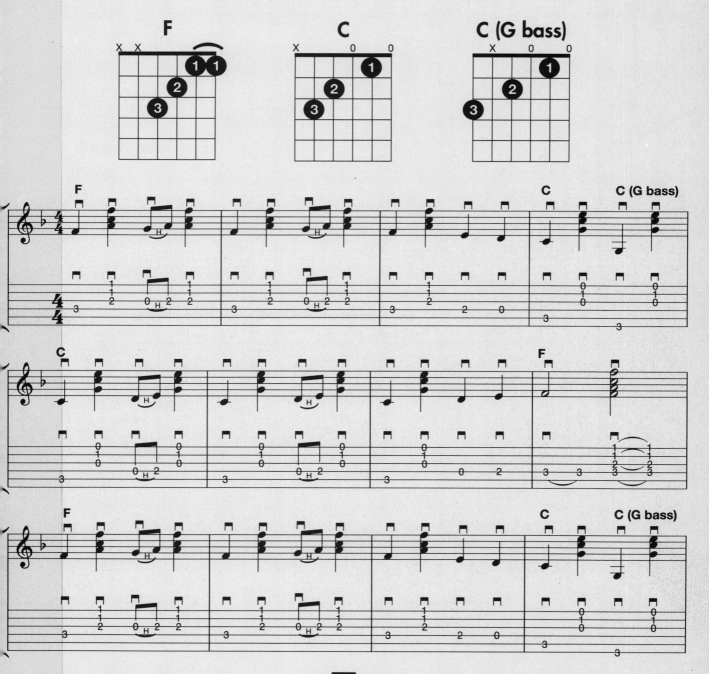

Lead guitar comes in (on the recording).

As you still have the pick in your hand, this is a good time to start playing some basic country lead guitar, starting with a G country scale and some picking exercises based around this and other scales. You will also get into slides, string bending and release string bending techniques, which will go further to adding a country sound to your playing.

Other techniques like combined flat picking fingerstyle and pedal steel effects will be introduced later in this book.

G MAJOR COUNTRY SCALE

The key of G is very good for playing country music and this simple G country scale is an ideal place to start. There are a few open strings here giving it a full 'ringy' sound. Just use downstrokes with the pick for the moment.

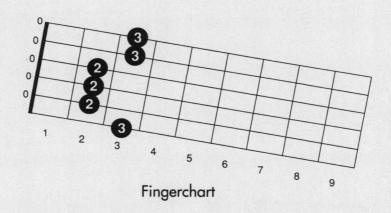

Fingerchart

12.

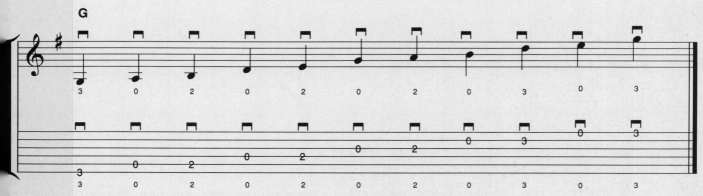

The left hand fingering is indicated by the numbers under each note.

PICKING EXERCISES BASED ON G COUNTRY SCALE

These three flat picking exercises are excellent for loosening up the left hand fingers, as well as developing the right-hand picking technique.

Practise slowly to start with. Try to play each note clearly and make full use of the open strings to attain a ringy sound.

13.

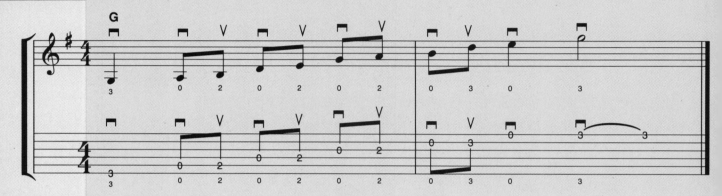

14.

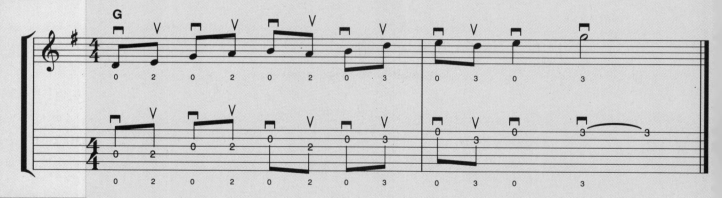

15.

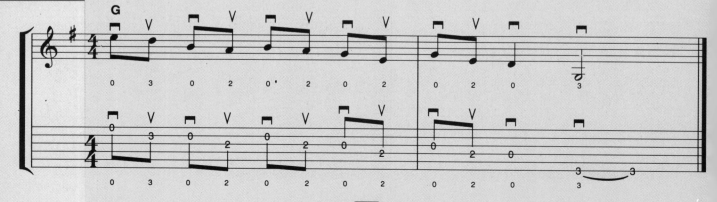

THE SLIDE

Incorporating slide techniques into your playing tends to smooth things out as well as making certain parts easier to play, so use these where ever you feel them necessary.

On this exercise place your 2nd finger (L.H.) on the 2nd fret of the 3rd string, strike the string and literally slide up to the 4th fret without striking again. Now try the next part of this exercise where you slide down from the 4th fret to the 2nd fret on the 3rd string.

16.

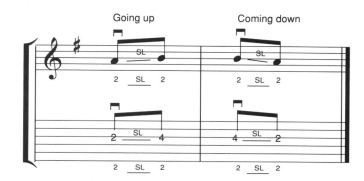

Try the following two guitar licks combining hammer-ons, pull-offs and slides.

17. G COUNTRY LICK

(NOTES FROM G COUNTRY SCALE)

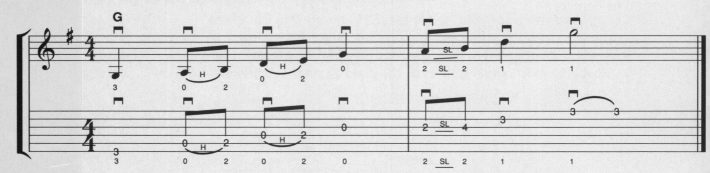

18. G COUNTRY LICK

(NOTES FROM G COUNTRY SCALE)

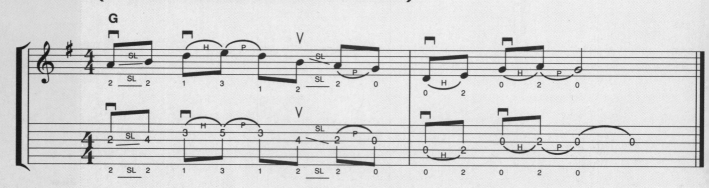

With these next three country guitar licks, we can start moving up along the fretboard.

19. COUNTRY LICK IN G

Notice the triplet starting with a slide in the third bar of each lick.

16

20. COUNTRY LICK IN A

We'll move up two frets now to raise the key to A. As there are no open strings in this, the L.H. fingering has changed accordingly.

The fingering is the same for the next lick as well.

21. COUNTRY LICK IN C

This lick moves along a further three frets to the key of C.

BY ALAN WARNER

This country guitar piece is fairly straight forward. Try taking it slowly, and learning it in sections. It is important to get the left-hand fingering right - correct positioning will make things easier for you.

Verse (Play verse three times)

Outro

Finger picking can provide all sorts of possibilities both for accompaniment and solo playing especially so for the 'Vamp' style. This is where the right hand thumb alternates from one string to another (usually 6th to 4th or 5th to 3rd strings) to a steady count of 1 2 3 4, whilst the right hand fingers pluck the other strings (usually treble strings).

There are other timings but as we're dealing with straight forward country music here we'll leave those out for the time being.

For the following exercise we will just concentrate on going from the 5th string to the 3rd string with the R.H. thumb. The P above the note indicates the thumb.

23. RIGHT HAND THUMB EXERCISE

(OPEN STRINGS)

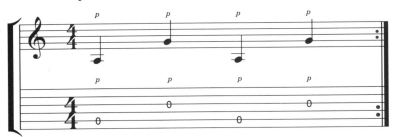

WAYLON JENNINGS (LFI)

Now try this exercise using thumb and fingers:
1) Strike the 5th string with the R.H. thumb (p) as before.
2) Then pluck the 1st string upwards with your R.H. middle finger (m).
3) Strike the 3rd string with the R.H. thumb (p) as before.
4) Pluck the 2nd string upwards with your R.H. index finger (i).

24. RIGHT HAND THUMB AND FINGER EXERCISE

(OPEN STRINGS)

Try this exercise again, this time using the C major chord.
This C major chord position will automatically provide the notes written on the musical notation and tablature.

25. RIGHT HAND THUMB AND FINGER EXERCISE

(USING C MAJOR CHORD)

FINGER PICKING EXERCISES

(VAMP STYLE)

These are the chords used for the following two exercises.

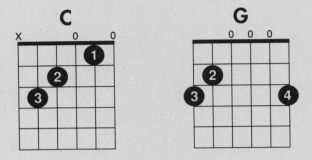

In this exercise when holding the C chord down your R.H. thumb alternates between the 5th and 3rd strings as it did on No. 25 on the previous page. On the G chord your thumb goes from the 6th to the 4th string.

26.

This exercise is more varied because in every other bar you pluck two strings together with your thumb and finger.

27.

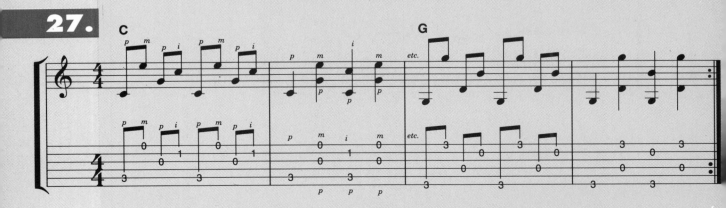

You will often find yourself having to modify chord shapes to conform to the musical structure of a vamp solo or accompaniment.

The following exercise gives you an example of this.

C

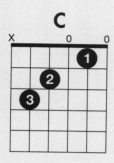

C (G treble note)

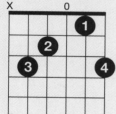 Add 4th finger

JAMES BURTON (LFI)

28.

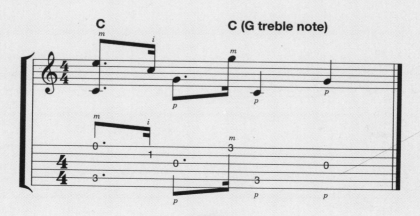

23

PREPARATION EXERCISES FOR CLEARWATER VAMP

We'll start preparing now for your first finger picking vamp solo. Study and practise the exercises laid out below.

Chord diagrams for the following preparation exercises for Clearwater Vamp

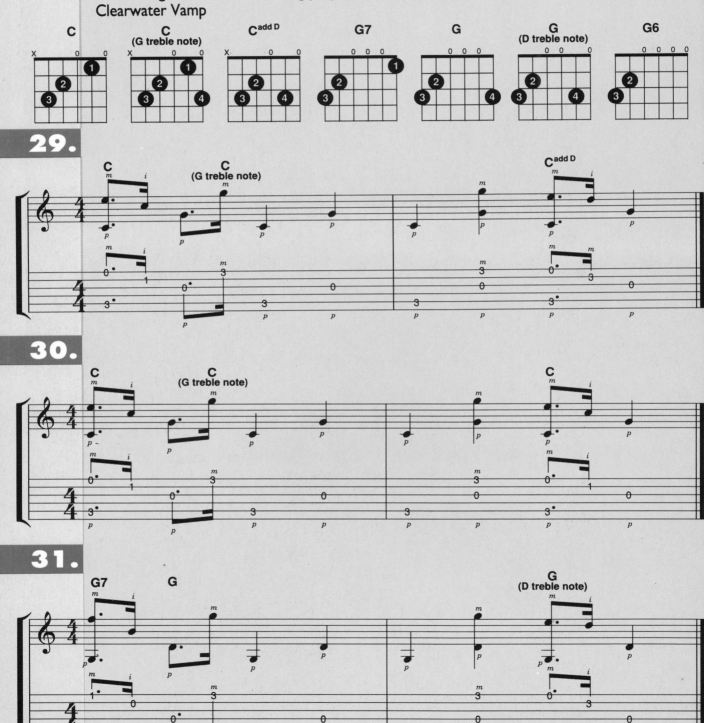

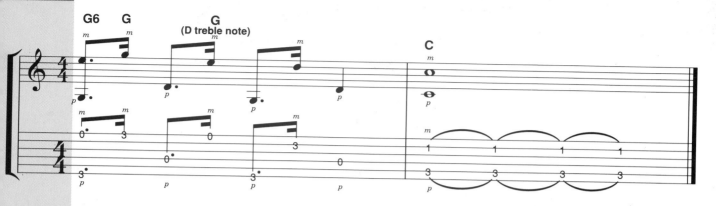

CARL PERKINS (PICTORIAL)

33. CLEARWATER VAMP

BY ALAN WARNER

34. CHORD SHAPES FOR RIVER VALLEY VAMP

All but three of the following chord shapes are quite straight forward. The chords F, F(♭5) and Dm are difficult because you need to hook your L.H. thumb over the 1st fret of the 6th string. There's no quick and easy way of getting used to this so you must practise hard.

C

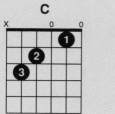

C^{add D}

F

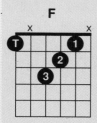

F(♭5)

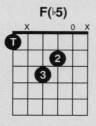

G

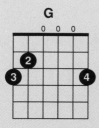

Dm

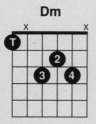

KRIS KRISTOFFERSON (LFI)

27

35. RIVER VALLEY VAMP

BY ALAN WARNER

I recorded this solo with a capo on the 5th fret to give it a 'sweeter' sound, so although I've written it in the key of C (without capo) the recorded version is in the key of F. Try experimenting with different capo positions.

*Notice I have introduced the ring finger = a, this plucks the 1st string.

28

ARPEGGIOS

The use of arpeggios can be quite effective in country music.
An arpeggio is a succession of notes from a chord played one after the other. Try the two arpeggio exercises below.

36. ARPEGGIO EXERCISE USING THE D CHORD

Once you have the D chord ready the picking procedure is:

4th string ⊓
3rd string ∨
2nd string ⊓
1st string ∨
2nd string ⊓
3rd string ∨
4th string ⊓

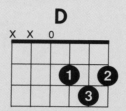

Keep going over this until you can play it fluently.

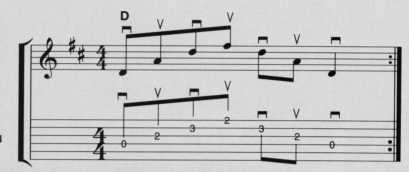

37. ARPEGGIO EXERCISE USING THE A CHORD

Once you have the A chord ready the picking procedure is:

5th string ⊓
3rd string ∨
2nd string ⊓
1st string ∨
2nd string ⊓
3rd string ∨
5th string ⊓

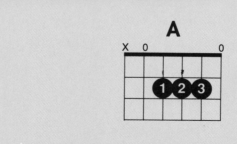

Keep going over this until you can play it fluently.

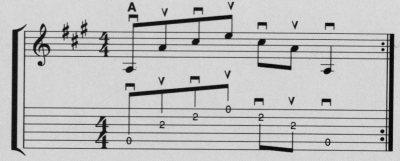

Try this arpeggio exercise. Note the hammer-on at the end of the 2nd and 6th bars, also at the end of the third bar you will need to lift your second finger off (open 4th string).
Remember to aim for a clean sound.

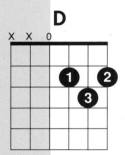

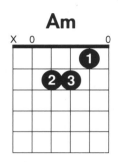

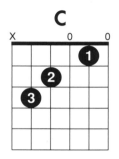

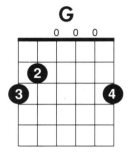

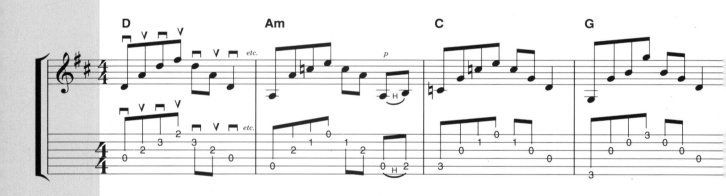

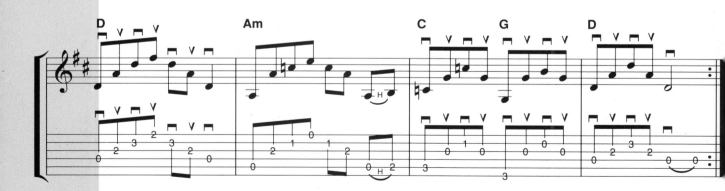

39. ARPEGGIO IN D

BY ALAN WARNER

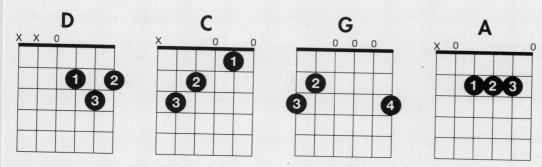

The arpeggios in this solo aren't quite so straight forward this time, so watch out for the hammer-on followed by a pull-off in bars 3, 12, 21 and 30.

Section 1

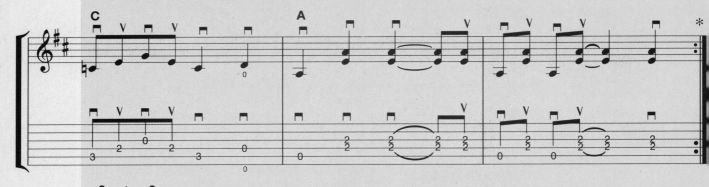

Section 2

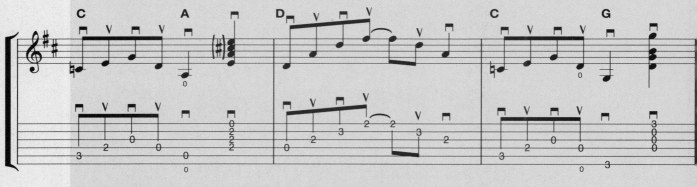

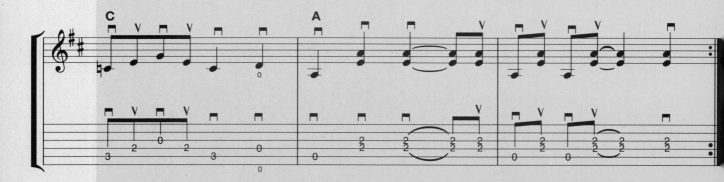

*Don't forget double lines and dots to repeat section.

40. G COUNTRY SCALE

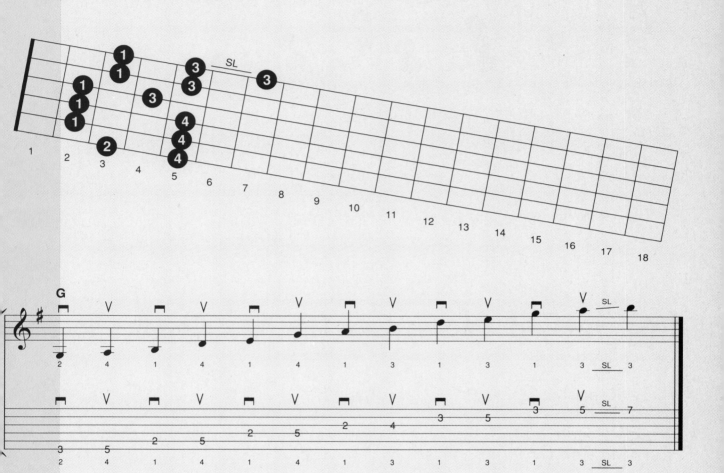

This scale uses the same notes as the scale on page 9 of this book, but this time the L.H. fingering is different because no open strings are used. There are also two extra notes added at the end, (5th fret to 7th fret of the 1st string.)

Now try this scale in the key of C.

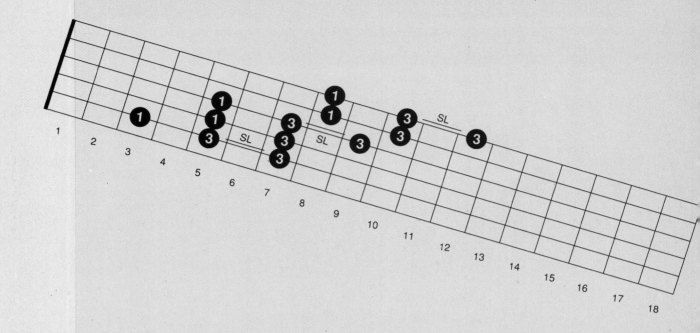

There are three slides in this scale: 5th fret to 7th fret of the 5th string, 7th fret to 9th fret of the 3rd string and the 10th fret to 12th fret of the 1st string.

BLUEGRASS STYLE
FLAT PICKING EXERCISES

42. This first exercise uses notes from the G major scale.
The notes are G A B C D E F# G

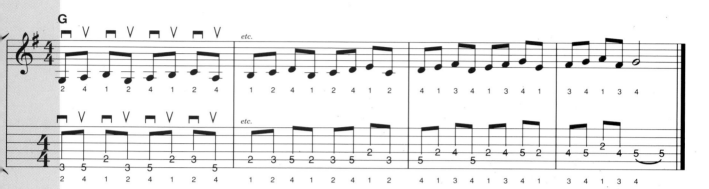

43. This exercise uses notes from the A major scale.
The notes are A B C# D E F# G# A

44. This exercise uses notes from the C major scale.
The notes are C D E F G A B C

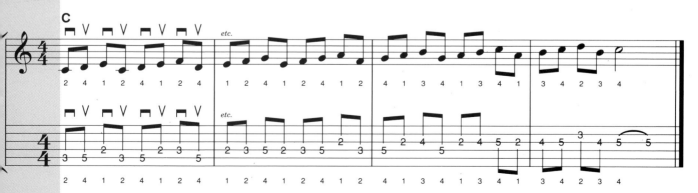

45. This exercise uses notes from the D major scale.
The notes are D E F#G A B C#D

In exercises 46 and 47 watch out for the 5th, 6th and 7th notes in bar 1. You'll have to stretch your L.H. fingers to manage them.

46.

47.

48.

49.

ELVIS PRESLEY, ON STAGE IN 1955 WITH SCOTTY MOORE (PICTORIAL)

50. BLUEGRASS GUITAR SOLO

BY ALAN WARNER

To play this solo through, play the sections in the following order:
1) Play section 1 three times.
2) Play section 2 twice.
3) Play section 1 and section 2 through without any repeats.
4) Finish off playing section 1 once.

Section 1

Section 2

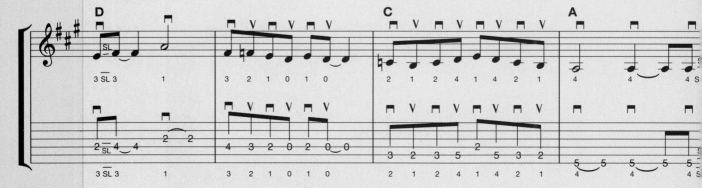

COMBINED FLAT PICKING FINGERSTYLE TECHNIQUES

Sound the two notes together with the pick and fingers on these double note scales.

51. C MAJOR COUNTRY SCALE (DOUBLE NOTE)

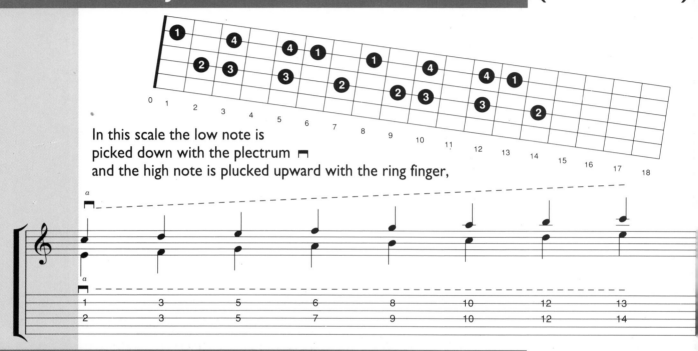

In this scale the low note is
picked down with the plectrum ⊓
and the high note is plucked upward with the ring finger,

52. G MAJOR COUNTRY SCALE (DOUBLE NOTE)

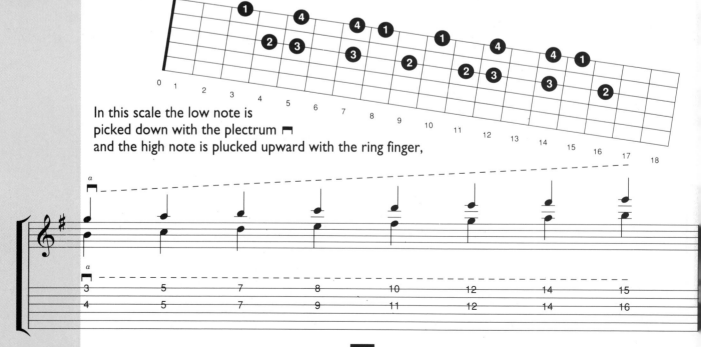

In this scale the low note is
picked down with the plectrum ⊓
and the high note is plucked upward with the ring finger,

53. COUNTRY LICK IN C

This lick uses notes from the C major (Double-note) country scale.

54. COUNTRY LICK IN G

This lick uses notes from the G major (Double-note) country scale (starts in D position).

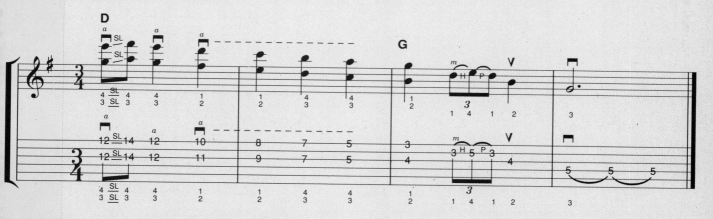

55. COUNTRY LICK IN G

56. 'BANJO' TYPE EXERCISE

57. 'BANJO' TYPE EXERCISE

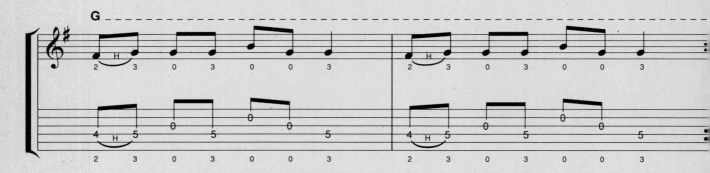

58. 'BANJO' TYPE LICK IN G

59. COUNTRY LICK IN G

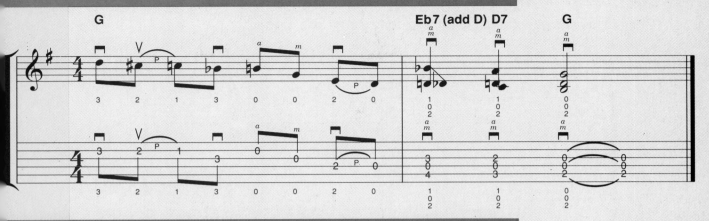

60. 'BANJO' TYPE LICK IN D

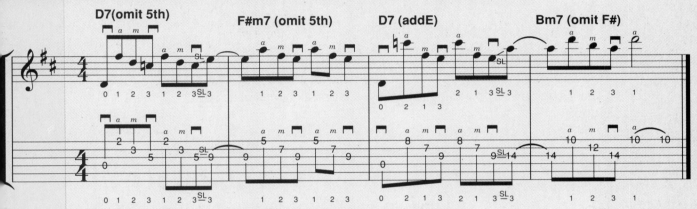

The use of open strings gives the following two licks a 'chime' effect

61. 'CHIME' LICK

62. 'CHIME' LICK

63. 'BANJO' TYPE LICK

Open strings are again used here, for a 'ringy' 'banjo' effect.

64. ROCKABILLY LICK IN E

Damp the 6th string slightly at the bridge with the heel of your right hand to give a muted effect. Also, if you have an effects unit, use a short slapback echo setting for an even more exciting rockabilly sound.

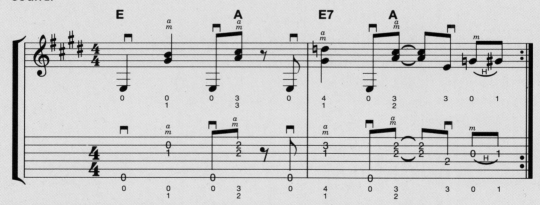

65. ROCKABILLY LICK IN A

Damp the 5th string for this lick, also use an echo effect if possible.

BASIC STRING BENDING TECHNIQUES

Another technique for country guitar is string bending or note bending. This is where you 'bend' the pitch up to a higher note instead of fretting that note. For example, if I wanted to bend from D to E on the second string I would sound the note (3rd fret/2nd string), strike the string then push the string hard upwards until the pitch becomes the same as the 5th fret. This would be known as a two-fret string bend because the notes are two frets apart.

66. TWO-FRET STRING BEND (UPWARDS)

Here's an illustration of this:

Use your 1st and 2nd fingers to reinforce the 3rd finger.

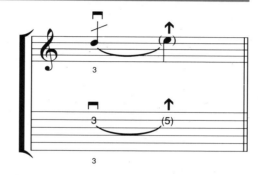

67. RELEASE BEND

Try adding a release bend to this. All you do here is simply release your finger back down to the D note.

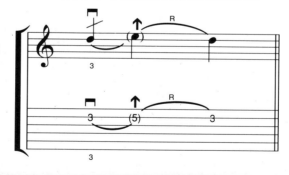

Bend string upwards as before.

Now release back to its original pitch.

68. ONE-FRET STRING BEND (DOWNWARDS)

Now try this one fret string bend. This time use your 1st finger to pull the string downwards.

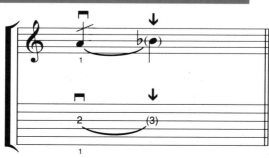

ADVANCED STRING BENDING TECHNIQUES

Before attempting any of the following string bending techniques, I strongly recommend that you try light gauge strings. I use .008, .011, .014, .022, .030 and .038, but you must experiment with different gauges if you wish to do so.

An exciting technique which is being used more and more by today's country players is the pedal steel effect. Take a look at the pedal steel exercise below. Form the first chord with your 3rd, 4th and 1st fingers, then sound the chord and bend the 3rd string down with your first finger. This will give you a two fret string bend. Follow this by a release bend back to the original note. Make sure that you keep your 3rd and 4th fingers firmly in place to allow the rest of the chord to ring on.

69. PEDAL STEEL EXERCISE

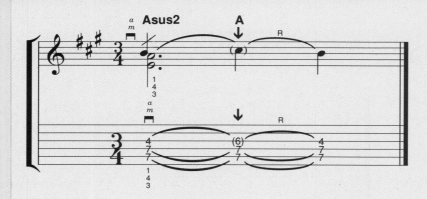

70. PEDAL STEEL LICK IN E

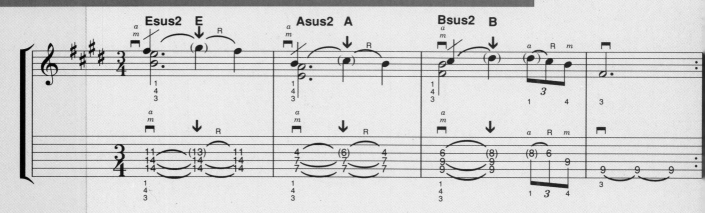

71. PEDAL STEEL LICK IN G

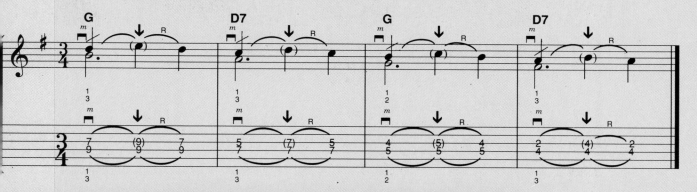

72. PEDAL STEEL LICK IN A

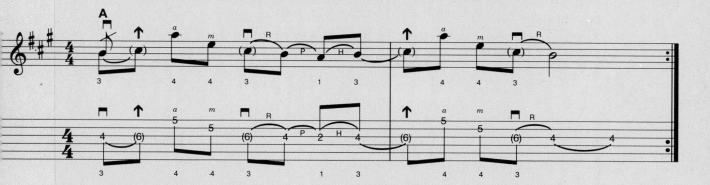

73. PEDAL STEEL LICK IN D

Watch out for the last bar of this lick: while the 3rd string is bent down catch the 7th fret note of the 2nd string and pluck the 2nd string. Then, while keeping your fingers on both strings, release back... Try it and see.

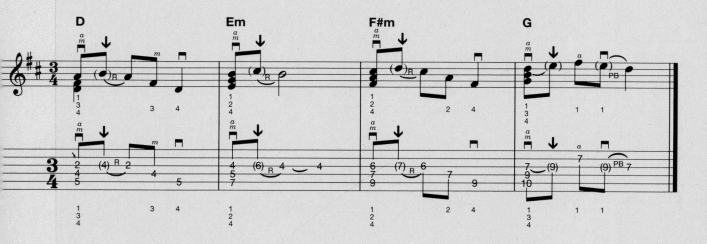

74. PEDAL STEEL LICK IN F

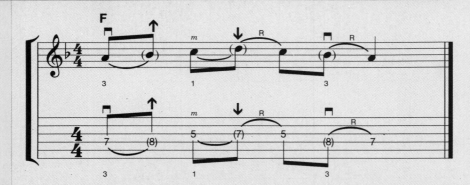

75. PEDAL STEEL LICK IN F

This lick starts the same as the previous lick, only this time when you bend the 3rd string down catch the 5th fret note of the 2nd string. Then push both strings up so the 2nd string note is raised by one semitone (one fret) and the 3rd string note is released back to its original note.

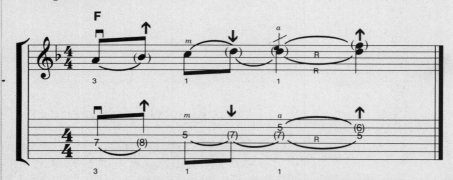

76. PEDAL STEEL LICK IN C

Although starting on an F major chord, this lick is in the key of C.

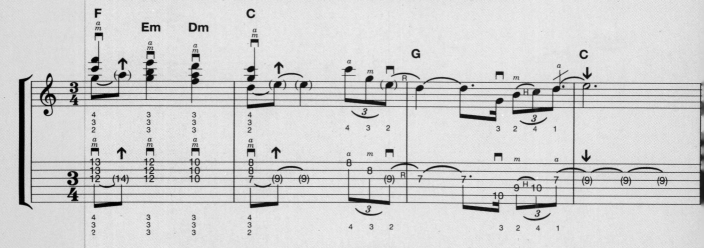